Easyread Java Interview Questions - Part 1

Malay Mandal

'no such thing as a stupid question'
— *Really? Have you ever attended a technical interview?*

Table of Contents

About the book

Targeted readership

This is not a book on learning Java. But it discusses interview questions. This may be helpful for interviewers, as well as potential candidates preparing for job interview, where Java questions may be asked. It focuses on core Java but also has questions on topics such as design pattern, which may be asked in a Java interview.

This may also help professionals who have been working in Java in a sense that certain questions may inspire them to fill up the gaps in topics they did not touch upon at all (or in detail). It may also help them with certain subtle understanding, which can help them improve the quality of code they write, as well as prepare them for interviews even in somewhat distant future.

Perhaps in rare cases, it may inspire people to plunge into further investigation of certain topic or aspect, which may pave the way for more complete knowledge.

Coverage

This book covers certain (but not all) Core Java topics. I have mainly used Java 1.7 for testing, and the code given here should be compatible to that (unless I have made a human error). It also has questions on topics such as design pattern, which may be asked in a Java interview. In that sense it could provide many *somewhat* complete set of questions for an interviewer.

Readability

This is a subjective judgement, but I have attempted to introduce questions in an easily readable fashion, with usually some little discussion on the main point of contention and the answer. Many questions are multiple choice or true/false type. In my view it should not take too long to read, (and possibly not too strenuous too). It is also suitable (in my view) for quick recap, perhaps on the day before the interview.

Stories! Really!

Let me start the book in earnest with some anecdotes. Related or unrelated. With the disclaimer, that they are work of fiction (which as fictions often do, may have been inspired, in parts, by real life events or characters – but they are nonetheless works of fiction), and should be treated as such.

1.   UltaVision Corporation is not doing well in terms of it's bottom-line. It didn't incur any loss this year, but the profit isn't good enough to justify the salary of it's CEO Mr. Homra Chomra in the eyes of the shareholders. He has asked the head of HR, Ms. Gunabati Shoemacher to come up with a plan, and she did. Even though they don't have a technical position, she put up ads for three technical position for senior people in their career page. Java Developer, Solutions Architect and Project Manager. To any unsuspecting bystander, it may appear, the company is going to carry out new project. From there people would possibly figure out, that they are expanding their operations (after all people are smart). That will eventually reflect in higher share prices (or so goes the thinking of Ms. Shoemacher).

2.   Tando has recently migrated to Australia. He is Java developer. Not a genius, but he can manage writing productive code for normal project, without much supervision. He needs a job. He applied through an internet job board to many positions, but of the few agents that got back to him at all, all are saying that he is not a close match for the jobs and they have better matches. He is a bit dumbfounded. In at least 3 jobs he would have thought he covered around 80% of the criteria. Surely a good programmer can pick up some extra bits and pieces on the job!

He called a friend, who came a few years ago, and is already settled here. In course of their conversation, he mentioned his predicament. And his friend gave him an idea.

Friend : "Do you think they go through all Cvs themselves. People sometimes apply just to gauge the market. Some people even apply for fun."

Tando : "How do they filter the Cvs then?"

Friend : "They have softwares, that look for keyword. Just cut the whole job description from the advertisement and paste it in the second page of your CV. Then save the CV and apply for the job. See what happens."

Tando could not respond immediately. He was somewhat lost.

Friend : " Don't forget to keep a copy of your original CV secure. Do not send a CV with two different advertisement together."

Tando : "No, No I won't do that." He was feeling somewhat uneasy in the stomach.

But later in the day, thinking what his wife will say, if he could not land a job soon, he had chosen a couple of jobs, and did as his friend suggested. Within the next hour he got calls for short-listing for both the jobs.

3.   Keralio was a bright student in his youth. He passed out of a prestigious engineering college with first class honours and joined a quiet lucrative junior position in a big organization (as a software developer). He was doing well in his career. But trouble started after his marriage.

He was never good at cooking or negotiation at shopping. Being street smart was not exactly his forte, but his academic intelligence and other qualities, more than compensated for that. Nobody in his family seemed to be bothered by that (before his marriage that is).

His wife expected the best of both worlds from him, and she demanded it. A small mistake that he may have made in housework, quiet often would have blown out of proportion, and sometimes overshadowed all his brilliant achievements in life, including but not limited to, his gold medal for top overall score in his batch. Upon continual denial of appreciation, he became irritable and somewhat vengeful. This was not part of his nature (at least in his earlier years).

He now works as a solutions architect in Chotokhato Corporation. There is a requirement for a Java Developer in the company, and he has been tasked with the technical part of the interview.

He does not have many place in life to release his anger, that is bottling up in him. If he gets into a physical fight with another guy in the street, chance is that he will get badly hurt. Not to mention any potential problem with the police. A candidate for a job interview, in a cool air-conditioned room, completely at his mercy (or so he thought), is a completely different scenario.

He started preparing his set of questions well.

4.   Rulik was driving taxi in the city. But lately there is not enough profit in that. Besides income tax department is getting harder on those cash deals.

He decided to join software development. He had a certificate course in software development few years back. He brushed up on that and applied for a project manager position. After all it won't require much technical skills. And as far as people management skills were concerned – well he had plenty of it, you bet. Getting short-listed was easy, he did some cut pasting from the job advertisement.

The HR personnel from the hiring company came back. They needed a reference from his earlier manager. He already thought through the scenario. And like an efficient manager (but not necessarily a conscientious one), he arranged to mitigate the risk by providing Mr. Tote Gulbaaj as his primary reference. Tote was a project manager for software projects in a small but somewhat known organization.

The HR Person Ms. Stunned called Tote, and asked about Rulik. The conversation went on for more than half an hour. And by the time it ended, Ms. Stunned were so impressed with Rulik's skill set, that she decided to take him on board even without a proper technical interview. There would be an interview though, but that is more a formality for onboarding (after all why waste time arranging technical interview for someone who is going to be an asset anyway).

5.   Mr Maradona (not the footballer., and Mr. Alvin Maradona is not a relation of him either), has never played soccer in his adult life. But he is a gifted and dedicated software developer. He tries to improve his knowledge continuously. Sometimes, he thinks about improving his code, even outside his office hours.

As a result of his recent thoughts, he created some generic class and used them in an innovative way to accomplish certain tasks (3 of them to be precise) in 6 hours each, which were originally estimated for 40 hours each. That is finishing a job in 15% of the estimated time.

This spelt doom for his immediate manager. You might think a manager would be happy if job gets done quickly. Think again. In a software development project, possibly one of the few skills expected from a manager, is the capability to estimate development time.

Now estimation may not always be accurate, but when it goes wrong in a ratio of 6:40, (and repeatedly so) that may raise serious question mark on the capability of the estimator.

Mr. Huffman (not the creator of the famous algorithm), Alvin's manager, decided it's time to get rid of him. He soon found a suitable opportunity. One module, in which Alvin worked before and which was in SIT, had an error found one day. Alvin fixed it. A week later another error cropped up. But who cares if it is another error. To the top level manager only numbers matter (at least that's what Mr. Huffman thought).

He promptly called a performance review meeting, involving Alvin and HR, in which all the complaints against him were hidden from him until he entered the meeting room.

"He said he fixed the error, but it was not fixed. He is very inefficient." The manager said. Before Alvin could open his mouth, the manager added "He did finish certain tasks quickly but that was repetitive."

Alvin tried to speak in his defence "But it is another error, not the original one. That error is ..". He was interrupted abruptly.

Manager : "We are giving you an option to improve your performance or to resign. If you take the first option we will have another review meeting after two weeks."

Alvin : "But I did work efficiently. I finshed those tasks in 15% of their..." he was cut short again.

Manager : "That was repetitive."

Alvin thought for a moment to point out, that those were deemed repetitive only from the point he created a generic solution for them. The original estimator did not estimate them as repetitive tasks. But something in him revolted.

Alvin : "Madam (addressing the HR lady), I think I am working quite efficiently, and I do not have much more room for improvement."

HR lady : "Well Mr. Maradona, in that case ..."

...

Stories are stories. They might be read for amusement. Why scratch your head on whether something like that ever happened.

Two main gate

Is it possible

This is a narrative that isn't entirely a work of fiction. However some of the details are difficult to recall from memory, and hence I will take the liberty to add and modify bits and pieces and present it like a story (although spoken in first person).

In not very recent past, I was looking for a job, and possibly as part of a short-listing process I had to take an online technical test on Core Java.

I am a postgraduate engineer, and I had quite a few years of Java development experience by then, most of it with big companies. Although I didn't know all the nuances of Java technology (and I still do not, although my knowledge has improved in the subject since then), I had a kind of confidence that I could write successful and productive code in Java, for any normal commercial project. Eventually how difficult can an online test be! After all it is Java.

I started my laptop and prepared to take the test.

After a while (possibly this was not the first question) I got a question somewhat like below.

If you run the code below what would be the result ?

```
//----------------------------
public class Test {
  public static void main(String args) {
    System.out.println("From main thread : " + 3 + 4);
  }

  public static void main(String[] args) {
    System.out.println("From main thread : " + 1 + 2);
  }
}
//----------------------------
```

And the alternatives -
(a) does not compile

(b) throws a runtime error

(c)　　runs and produces

From main thread : 12

(d)　　runs and produces

From main thread : 7

From main thread : 3

This was new to me. In all my years of productive programming (till that point), I have never thought of writing two main methods in a Java class. Why on earth would somebody do that ?

But in an interview (a job interview) you are supposed to answer questions not ask them.

[To set one matter aside. The correct choice is (c)]

For better or for worse -

(1)　　An interview may or may not be about what you have done ?

(2)　　More surprisingly perhaps, it may not be about what the job requires ? [It is quite likely that someone who hasn't fared well in the interview, is more than capable to carry out the job].

(3)　　It may be argued that you should be pushed to the limit so that the best of you comes out. And this may be true at least in some cases. However it is possible that by asking questions that, at least in terms of subtlety, that has no bearing on the duties to be performed, the interviewer is trying to gratify his ego. But for the candidate, it boils down to (under normal circumstances) a matter of screening.

(4)　　Some questions may be asked purely to make the candidate uncomfortable (whatever be the stated reason behind them). For the sake of fairness, you would expect that such effort be made with all the candidates, and you are not the only one singled out for such advance. However getting depressed, for not being able to answer one question towards the beginning, may cost heavily in performance for other questions where you could have answered well, if you had taken it easy.

"Take it easy" is a phrase in English which is "Easier said

than done" (another phrase), sometimes much easier said than done. You may have your own way to follow the advice. However taking a question critically, on it's technical merit, rather than the basing it on the motivation behind asking such a question, (however sinister that may be), may help in this regard.

...

I never encountered such a question before. However the question is about overloading methods, and quite a legitimate one. However much may be it's surprise value (to the interviewer). [This of course I did not realise during the test].

Since then I have appeared in quite a few technical tests and technical interviews. I was successful in many of them (not all). I studied a lot of interview questions. Quite often, tried to remember questions that were asked to me during an interview. Especially the one's I could not answer. And tried to search the answers from various sources, internet included.

This process made me more successful as a candidate. But I also realized, that a sort of opinion, that I held earlier (that these are not really required to carry out the job), is not entirely true. Learning about the nuances may change the thought process around designing a program. The outcome may be more robust or more efficient code.

I still do not accept that "There's no such thing as a stupid question". However recently I encountered another quotation, and I quite like it -

"I'd rather live with a good question than a bad answer"
- Aryeh A. Frimer

Questions in Earnest

FizzBuzz

I have encountered questions, similar to the one given below (Q2), a number of times. Sometimes such a question is asked even as part of the initial application (in Sydney, Australia).

Q2. Write a code (Java class) which will print integers from one to hundred to the console, except if the number is divisible by 3 then it would print "Fizz" if it is divisible by 5 then it would print "Buzz" and if it is divisible by both 3 and 5 then it would print "FizzBuzz"?

A. There isn't much trick involved in it. You need to know certain basic syntax, and you need to be careful to evaluate the divisible by both (3 and 5) case first to avoid any nasty surprise.

The following code will do nicely.

```
//---------------------------
public class Test {
    public static void main(String[] args) {
        for (int i = 1; i <= 100; i++) {
            if ((i % 15) == 0)
                System.out.println("FizzBuzz");
            else if ((i % 3) == 0)
                System.out.println("Fizz");
            else if ((i % 5) == 0)
                System.out.println("Buzz");
            else
                System.out.println("" + i);
        }
    }
}
//---------------------------
```

Note that in the last println statement I has been added to an empty String to make it a String concatenation (the result of which should be a String) because println takes a String argument.

Constructors vs methods

Q3a. what happens when you try to run the following -

```
//-----------------------------------
public class Test {

   public void Test() {
      System.out.println("Constructing Test ...");
   }

   public static void main(String[] args) {
      Test test = new Test();
      System.out.println("Running Test main ...");
   }

}
//-----------------------------------
```

    The set of alternatives
    (a) Does not compile successfully
    (b) runs and prints -
    Running Test main ...
    (c) runs and prints -
    Constructing Test ...
    Running Test main ...

    If you do not find any obvious error, or something that is strikingly unfamiliar in context, my advise is do not force yourself to invent a compilation error.

    The choice then narrows down to (b) and (c).

    It may be tempting to jump to the answer (c) because on a cursory glance, the code body immediately containing the first println statement seems to be the constructor.

The subtle difference between a constructor, and a method by the same name, is that the method has a return type and a constructor does not.

So that makes it a method. It means, in turn, that when the class is instantiated inside the main method, using a constructor, this method (being a method and not a constructor), will not be called. And hence any statement within the method will not be executed.

The correct answer then is (b).

And as a corollary, if you remove the *void* keyword from the first function definition, it will print two lines instead of 1 [as given in answer(c)]

A variation of the question with an important distinction is -

Q3b.

```
//----------------------------------
public class Test {

    public static void Test() {
        System.out.println("Constructing Test ...");
    }

    public static void main(String[] args) {
        Test test = new Test();
        System.out.println("Running Test main ...");
    }

}
```

```
//-----------------------------------
```
          The set of alternatives

          (a) Does not compile successfully

          (b) runs and prints -

          Running Test main ...

          (c) runs and prints -

          Constructing Test ...

          Running Test main ...

          At first glance the first method may be mistaken for a constructor. On top of that if you are in a dilemma as to whether you can define a static constructor, things get further complicated. But if you identify it as a method (which it is), you can easily deduce, that by the same line of reasoning (as the previous question), the correct answer will be (b).

Static constructor

Q4. For the following question however -

```java
//-----------------------------------
public class Test {
   public static Test() {
      System.out.println("Constructing Test ...");
   }

   public static void main(String[] args) {
      Test test = new Test();
      System.out.println("Running Test main ...");
   }
}
//-----------------------------------
```
          (given the same alternative as the previous question) the

debate turns around whether you can have a static constructor to a class.

Before answering the questions, think what a constructor means (not in copybook terms, but what it does). It is a part of instantiation (i.e. associated closely with an instance). Whereas static context is associated with the whole class irrespective of any instance. Constructor and static then should not go together.

Hence it is only reasonable that you can not have a static constructor. The correct answer is (a).

Default constructor

Q5a. How many constructor does this class have -

```
//-----------------------------------
public class Test {
    public static void main(String[] args) {
        Test.echo();
    }

    private static void echo() {
        System.out.println("Running Test ...");
    }
}
//-----------------------------------
```

The alternatives are -

(a) 0

(b) 1

(c) 2

The alternative (a) could be tempting. No constructor is defined within the code body, and no instance has been explicitly instantiated from within the code. It invokes a static method referring to the class, and it will run nicely.

However the catch is - *JVM provides a constructor (known as default constructor) for any class where an explicit constructor is not provided. That is a no argument public constructor.* So when the class is in action, it will actually have a constructor. The correct answer is (b).

On the same principle look at the following two questions -

Q5b. How many constructor does this class have -

```
//---------------------------------
public class Test {
  public Test() {}

  public static void main(String[] args) {
    Test.echo();
  }

  private static void echo() {
    System.out.println("Running Test ...");
  }
}
//---------------------------------
```

Q5c. and how many constructor does this class have -

```
//---------------------------------
public class Test {
  private int countIt;

  public Test(int countIt) {
    this.countIt = countIt;
  }
```

```
    public static void main(String[] args) {  }
}
//----------------------------------
```

In both cases the answer is 1. Because *the default constructor comes into play, only when there is no explicit constructor provided, with or without argument.*

Field

A slight digression now.

Q6a. What would the following result in -

```
//----------------------------------
public class Test {
    private int countIt;

    public Test() {
        this.countIt = 5;
    }

    public static void main(String[] args) {
        System.out.println("Count is : " + countIt);
    }
}
//----------------------------------
```

The set of alternatives

(a) Does not compile successfully

(b) runs and prints -

Count is : 5

(c) runs and prints -

Count is : 0

countIt is a member variable of the class (an instance variable and not a static one), hence must be accessed through an instance, not through a static context. the main method here being a static method, won't be able to use the variable without instantiating an object (and then using the instance). The right answer in this case is (a).

The above code can be changed slightly to access the variable for printing, in this way -

Q6b. What would the following result in -

```
//----------------------------------
public class Test {
    private int countIt;

    public Test() { this.countIt = 5; }

    public static void main(String[] args) {
        Test test = new Test();
        System.out.println("Count is : " + test.countIt);
    }
}
//----------------------------------
```

The set of alternatives

(a) Does not compile successfully

(b) runs and prints -

Count is : 5

(c) runs and prints -

Count is : o

The correct alternative here is (b).

Constructor chaining

Let's have some discussion on constructor chaining.

Java being an object oriented language, allows inheritance. One class can be extended by another. In such cases, what happens to the constructors during instantiation?

Consider the following code (which are written in three different files).

Q7. What will happen when class Test is attempted to run -

```
//-----------------------------------
public class Chld extends Parnt {
}

public class Parnt {
  public Parnt() {
    System.out.println("Constructing Parnt ...");
  }
}

public class Test {
  public static void main(String[] args) {
    new Chld();
    System.out.println("done ...");
  }
}
//-----------------------------------
```

The set of alternatives

(a) Does not compile successfully

(b) runs and prints -

Constructing Parnt ...

done ...

(c) runs and prints -

done ...

Clearly the focus here is whether the constructor of the Parnt class will be executed, even though it has not been explicitly invoked.

The answer is yes. and hence the correct choice in this case is (b).

It gets slightly more complicated when the child class constructor also does something explicit.

Q8. What will happen when Test class below is attempted to run?

```
//---------------------------------
public class Chld extends Parnt {
   public Chld() {
      System.out.println("Constructing Chld ...");
   }
}

public class Parnt {
   public Parnt() {
      System.out.println("Constructing Parnt ...");
   }
}

public class Test {
   public static void main(String[] args) {
      new Chld();
   }
}
```

```
//--------------------------------
        The set of alternatives
        (a) runs and prints -
        Constructing Chld ...
        (b) runs and prints -
        Constructing Chld ...
        Constructing Parnt ...
        (c) runs and prints -
        Constructing Parnt ...
        Constructing Chld ...
```

You can rule out the first choice as it has already been discussed that the constructor of the Parnt class will be invoked. The focus then is, in what order would the constructors of those two classes invoked. If you try to draw simile with the real world, where parent comes before child, (c) would be the sensible choice. And that is the correct one in this case.

What will happen if you change the signature of both the Parent constructor, and child constructor like -

Q9.

```
//--------------------------------
public class Chld extends Parnt {
    public Chld(int count) {
        System.out.println("Constructing Chld ...");
    }
}

public class Parnt {
    public Parnt(int count) {
        System.out.println("Constructing Parnt ...");
```

```
    }
}

public class Test {
    public static void main(String[] args) {
        new Chld();
    }
}
//---------------------------------
```
Will result in -
(a) Does not compile successfully
(b) runs and prints -
Constructing Chld ...
Constructing Parnt ...
(c) runs and prints -
Constructing Parnt ...
Constructing Chld ...

Well, no matter what the set of arguments of the child class constructor is, if a particular constructor of the parent class is not explicitly called, JVM will always try to call a no argument constructor on the parent class, while instantiating the parent. In this case, since the class Parnt already have a constructor, the default constructor will not be supplied. Hence no constructor with no argument (without any argument) will be available. And hence an attempt to instantiate the Chld class this way will result in compilation error. The correct choice is therefore (a).

It would be an altogether different matter if you were to call the specific constructor of the Parnt class using super keyword, in the constructor of Chld.
The following code for Chld will run nicely in this case

```
//-------------------------------
public class Chld extends Parnt {
   public Chld() {
      super(0);
      System.out.println("Constructing Chld ...");
   }
}
//-------------------------------
```
and produce

Constructing Parnt ...
Constructing Chld ...

Q10. What about the following code -
```
//-------------------------------
public class Chld extends Parnt {
   public Chld() {
      System.out.println("Constructing Chld ...");
      super(0);
   }
}
//-------------------------------
```
Will result in -

(a) Does not compile successfully

(b) runs and prints -

Constructing Chld ...

Constructing Parnt ...

(c) runs and prints -

Constructing Parnt ...

Constructing Chld ...

Note that super, when used, should always be the first statement in the child classes constructor body. Hence the above code will result in compile time error. Correct alternative then is (a).

Q11. Since we are at it, what will the following result in ?

```
//---------------------------------
public class Chld extends Parnt {
    public Chld() {
        System.out.println("Constructing Chld ...");
    }

    public void echo() {
        super();
    }
}

public class Parnt {
    public Parnt() {
        System.out.println("Constructing Parnt ...");
    }
}

public class Test {
    public static void main(String[] args) {
        Chld chld = new Chld();
        chld.echo();
    }
}
//---------------------------------
```

The set of alternatives

(a) Does not compile successfully

(b) runs and prints -

Constructing Parnt ...

Constructing Chld ...

Constructing Parnt ...

(c) runs and prints -

Constructing Parnt ...

Constructing Chld ...

The keyword super is meant to invoke the constructor of the parent class. It is only fair, that that should not be used once the parent class is already constructed. Hence *the use of super, in a method of the child class (and not a constructor), is not allowed.* This will result in compile time error. Choice (a).

Q12. What, however, will the following code result in ?

```
//-----------------------------------
public class Chld extends Parnt {
    public Chld() {
        System.out.println("Constructing Chld ...");
    }

    public void echo() {
        new Parnt();
    }
}

public class Parnt {
    public Parnt() {
```

```
        System.out.println("Constructing Parnt ...");
    }
}


public class Test {
    public static void main(String[] args) {
        Chld chld = new Chld();
        chld.echo();
    }
}
//----------------------------------
```

The set of alternatives

(a) Does not compile successfully

(b) runs and prints -

Constructing Parnt ...

Constructing Chld ...

Constructing Parnt ...

(c) runs and prints -

Constructing Parnt ...

Constructing Chld ...

In this case, a new instance of Parnt (other than the one being instantiated implicitly from the constructor of the Chld class) is being instantiated from the echo method. Which will result in a third print statement after the statement from the child class constructor. The correct alternative is (b).

Range overrun

Enough of constructors. Let's explore another area.

Q13. Given - a byte has a range of -128 to 127 (both values

included), what will the following code result in -

```
//-----------------------------------
public class Test {
    public static void main(String[] args) {
        byte x = 128;
        System.out.println("value of x is : " + x);
    }
}
//-----------------------------------
```

The set of alternatives

(a) Does not compile successfully

(b) runs and prints -

value of x is : 128

(c) runs and prints -

value of x is : 127

The underlying question is, *if in the initial assignment, a variable is attempted to be assigned a value beyond it's range, will it throw an error, or will it take the largest value that it can. (Or is there any other possibility?)* . In this case it throws a compilation error. The correct answer is (a).

Would it have a made a difference if the assignment was made an expression? such as 120 + 8; The answer is no.

Q14. However what will happen to the following code ?

```
//-----------------------------------
public class Test {
    public static void main(String[] args) {
        byte x = 127;
        System.out.println("value of x is : " + x);
        x++;
```

```
        System.out.println("value of x is : " + x);
    }
}
//----------------------------------
```

        The set of alternatives

        (a) Does not compile successfully
        (b) runs and prints -
        value of x is : 127
        value of x is : -128
        (c) results in exception at runtime

        In this case it actually runs and prints values as given in
alternative (b);

        However note that the following -
```
//----------------------------------
public class Test {
    public static void main(String[] args) {
        byte x = 127;
        System.out.println("value of x is : " + x);
        x = x + 1;
        System.out.println("value of x is : " + x);
    }
}
//----------------------------------
```
results in a compile time error.

        In the case of the increment operator, I suspect, since the
increment happens in-situ, somehow it is done shifting the bits
(and not as an assignment). However assignments with

expressions, whose value is known at compile time to be beyond the range, is not accepted.

Operator

A change of taste.

Q15. With respect to the following code -

```
//----------------------------------
public class Test {
    public static void main(String[] args) {
        int x = 5;
        System.out.println("x = " + --x + 1);
        System.out.println("x = " + x++ + 1);
    }
}
//----------------------------------
```

will it print

x = 5

x = 5

(a) true

(b) false

The answer is false (or no). One temptation here is to focus on the prefix and postfix operation, and try to deduce whether x is incremented, or decremented before the print or after the print. However depending on how quickly you jump to conclusion, you may or may not guess what it exactly prints. Which is -

x = 41

x = 41

There are few catches here. One is that, *all the + operators are actually on strings (so concatenation)*. The other is that, *even if 1 were to be added to x as an integer operation, the result is still not being assigned to x*, hence the addition would not have altered the value of x (the value in the registry location, pointed to by x).

However the string concatenation part can be easily changed by using a few parentheses.

Q16. And what will the following result in ?

```
//----------------------------------
public class Test {
    public static void main(String[] args) {
        int x = 5;
        System.out.println("x = " + (--x + 1));
        System.out.println("x = " + (x++ + 1));
    }
}
//----------------------------------
```

The set of alternatives

(a) runs and prints

x = 5

x = 6

(b) will print

x = 41

x = 51

(c) will print

x = 5

x = 5

And here is where your prefix, postfix argument should come into play (if you were planning to argue on that line, that is).

The correct choice here is (c).

instance of

Coming to instanceof check -

Q17. What will the following result in ?

```
//----------------------------------
public class Test {
    public static void main(String[] args) {
        String str = null;
        if (str instanceof String)
            System.out.println("Null is a string");
        else
            System.out.println("Null is not a string");
    }
}
//----------------------------------
```

The set of alternatives
(a) Does not compile successfully
(b) results in NullPointerException at runtime
(c) runs and prints -
Null is not a string

In my view the main point of contention here is, *whether instanceof check can be applied to a null object*. It turns out that it is legal. To the extent that the '*if*' line in the above code could have been replaced by -

if (null instanceof String)

and that would still be legal. The correct answer in this case is (c).

Initialisers

Q18. The following code will result in ?

```
//----------------------------------
public class Test {
   private static int i = 1;
   { i = 2; }
   static { i = 3; }

   public static void main(String[] args) {
      System.out.println("i = " + i);
      Test test = new Test();
      System.out.println("i = " + i);
   }
}
//----------------------------------
```

The set of alternatives

(a) Does not compile successfully

(b) runs and prints -

i = 1

i = 2

(c) runs and prints -

i = 3

i = 2

Before answering the question, let me discuss a slight variation to the above, where the static block is taken out. i.e.

Q19.

```
//----------------------------------
public class Test {
   private static int i = 1;
```

```java
    { i = 2; }

    public static void main(String[] args) {
        System.out.println("i = " + i);
        Test test = new Test();
        System.out.println("i = " + i);
    }
}
//---------------------------------
```

       Will result in -

       (a) Does not compile successfully

       (b) runs and prints -

       i = 1

       i = 2

       (c) runs and prints -

       i = 3

       i = 2

Both the above questions has to do with the order in which blocks and static field initialisation takes place for a class. Any value that is assigned at declaration itself is possibly assigned during loading the class, and then overwritten by the static initialiser block. The unnamed block (but not static) fires apparently during object instantiation. So any initial assignment on declaration (for static variables), will be modified by static block (if assigned there), and further modified by initializer block for objects when the object initialises.

In the first instance, the first print happens before object instantiation, hence it should have value assigned at static initialiser block. The next print happens after object instantiation and hence will carry value from unnamed initializer block. The correct answer is (c).

In the second question, the static initialiser block is not present. Hence the first print has value from the initial assignment (not overwritten by static initialiser). The second print has value as assigned from unnamed initializer block. The correct answer in this case is (b).

However given a static initializer block but not the unnamed (object level) initialiser block, the following will result in -

```
//----------------------------------
public class Test {
    private static int i = 1;
    static { i = 3; }
    public static void main(String[] args) {
        System.out.println("i = " + i);
        Test test = new Test();
        System.out.println("i = " + i);
    }
}
//----------------------------------
```

a print of -

i = 3

i = 3

The next question is on operator semantics.

Q20. What would be the outcome of attempting to run the following ?

```
//----------------------------------
public class Test {
    public static void main(String[] args) {
```

```
        byte i = 2;
        if ((i > 1) ^ (i > 0))
            System.out.println("whatever");
        else
            System.out.println("got it");
    }
}
//----------------------------------
```

The set of alternatives

(a) Does not compile successfully

(b) runs and prints -

whatever

(c) runs and prints -

got it

The code will not pose any compilation problem. It uses a logical operator ^ which represents an exclusive or. Which works differently from the other or (|) in the sense that it will be true when one of the expression on either side is true, and the other is false. It won't evaluate to true if both are true.

But in case of this question both the expressions presented to it are true, so it will evaluate to false. The correct choice is (c).

Flow of control

Q21. What will the following result in -

```
//----------------------------------
public class Test {
    public static void main(String[] args) {
        boolean i = false;
```

```
   while (i = true) {
       System.out.println("inside while : " + i);
   }
  }
}
```
//-----------------------------------

The set of alternatives

(a) Does not compile successfully

(b) runs and prints in infinite loop
inside while : false

(c) runs and prints in infinite loop
inside while : true

(d) runs but does not print anything

Notice that the part inside the condition of while is not i == true (which would evaluate to false) but i = true. Since while takes a boolean (or boolean expression) as a condition, this would have resulted in a compilation error had you tried it with an int (e.g. i = 2) for instance.

However any valid assignment statement has a value. The value is - what gets assigned to the left hand side of the statement after computing the RHS expression. Hence in this case, the whole assignment will evaluate to true (the value of i upon assignment). Hence the while will be an infinite loop (and i will be assigned to true from the condition). The correct answer is (c).

Switching to questions of switch -

Q22a. Which of the types are not supported by the switch statement ?

(a) byte

(b) short

(c) int

(d) long

And another variation to the same question

Q22b. Which of the types are supported by the switch statement -

(a) byte

(b) Byte

(c) char

(d) Enum

(e) all of the above

For the first question the answer is (d). long is perhaps too big to handle for an option of switch statement.

For the second question both Enum and wrapper class of byte (as well as wrapper classes for char, short and int) are supported by switch statement. So the answer is (e).

Q23. What will the following result in -

```
//-----------------------------------
public class Test {
    public static void main(String[] args) {
        int i;

        for (i = 11; i < 10; i++)
            i = 2 * i;

        System.out.println("i = " + i);
    }
}
```

//----------------------------------

The set of alternatives

(a) Does not compile successfully

(b) runs and prints -

i = 22

(c) runs and prints -

i = 11

The main point of contention here is whether *'for'* will evaluate the exit condition even before the first execution of it's loop. (i.e. will it go the while way or the do-while way). *'for'* actually checks the exit condition even before the first run of the loop. Hence (c) is the correct answer here.

Q24. What will the following result in ?
//----------------------------------

```
public class Test {
   public static void main(String[] args) {

      int i,j,k;
      String rslt = "";

      for(i = 1; i <= 2; i++) {
         rslt = rslt + "i" + i;
         then:
         for(j = 1; j <= 3; j++) {
            rslt = rslt + "j" + j;
            for(k = 1; k <= 4; k++) {
               rslt = rslt + "k" + k;
               break then;
```

```
            }
          }
        }


      System.out.println(rslt);
    }
  }
//----------------------------------
```

alternatives

(a) Does not compile successfully

(b) runs and prints -

i1j1k1k2k3k4j2k1k2k3k4

(c) runs and prints -

i1j1k1i2j1k1

This is to do with labelled for loops, which are perhaps not in common use. The code will compile correctly and the right answer is (c). As soon as the break statement is hit, it will break to the label then: and the outer *for* still has one more looping left when that label is first escaped to. Note that *then* is not a keyword in Java.

Q25. What will the following result in ?

```
//----------------------------------
public class Test {
    public static void main(String[] args) {

      int i,j,k;
      String rslt = "";

      for(i = 1; i <= 2; i++) {
```

```
        rslt = rslt + "i" + i;
        elseif:
        for(j = 1; j <= 2; j++) {
            rslt = rslt + "j" + j;
            for(k = 1; k <= 2; k++) {
                rslt = rslt + "k" + k;
                continue elseif;
            }
        }
    }

    System.out.println(rslt);
  }
}
//---------------------------------
```

alternatives

(a) Does not compile successfully

(b) runs and prints -

i1j1k1i2j1k1

(c) runs and prints -

i1j1k1j2k1i2j1k1j2k1

This is code with labelled continue and the correct answer is (c). Note that *elseif* (a single word) is not a keyword in Java.

Variable declaration

Q26. About the following variable declarations, please choose the right alternative -

int $i;

(a) valid

(b) invalid starts with $

int sa123456789012345678901234567890;
     (a) valid
     (b) invalid more than 30 characters long

int 1a;
     (a) valid
     (b) invalid start with a digit.

It is perfectly legal, although not advisable to start a variable name with $. [Underscore also is a valid starting character for variable names]

It is also legal to have a variable name more than 30 characters long. There is no limit of length.

However you can not start a variable name with a digit. So the correct choices are (a),(a), and (b) respectively.

Access

Q27. How many different types of access a class member can have in Java?

A. 4. public, protected, private and default (when nothing is specified).

Q28. What is the access domain for a default variable.

A. within the package

String

Q29. What will be the outcome of the following ?

```
//---------------------------------
public class Test {
```

```java
    private String str = "";
    public static void main(String[] args) {
        String str = " world";
        str.trim();
        System.out.println("Hello" + str);
    }
}
//----------------------------------
```

The set of alternatives

(a) runs and prints -

Hello

(b) runs and prints -

Hello world

(c) runs and prints -

Helloworld

The local variable within the main function will take precedence over the field. (In fact if the local variable declaration is not there, it will result in a compilation error, as non-static field will in that case, be used in a static context). String str is being trimmed, however the result of the operation is not being stored anywhere. Remember String is an immutable class. So the original String (str) will still retain it's initial value. Hence the correct answer is (b).

However if you were to do the trim within the print statement, i.e.

```java
    System.out.println("Hello" + str.trim());
```

that would result in a string Helloworld (without a blank space) being printed.

What would be the outcome in each of the following cases ?

Q30a.

```java
//--------------------------------
public class Test {
    public static void main(String[] args) {
        String str1 = "hello";
        String str2 = new String("hello");
        if (str1 == str2)
            System.out.println("equal");
        else
            System.out.println("not equal");
    }
}
//--------------------------------
```

alternatives
(a) prints
equal
(b) prints
not equal

Q30b.

```java
//--------------------------------
public class Test {
    public static void main(String[] args) {
        String str1 = "hello";
        String str2 = "hello";
        if (str1 == str2)
            System.out.println("equal");
        else
            System.out.println("not equal");
```

```
      }
}
//---------------------------------
```

alternatives
(a) prints
equal
(b) prints
not equal

Q30c.
```
//---------------------------------
public class Test {
   public static void main(String[] args) {
      String str1 = "hello";
      String str2 = new String("hello");
      if (str1.equals(str2))
         System.out.println("equal");
      else
         System.out.println("not equal");
   }
}
//---------------------------------
```

alternatives
(a) prints
equal
(b) prints
not equal

In the first case, it would print 'not equal' and in other 2 cases, 'equal'. String class maintains a pool of objects (Strings), and when a literal is used to assign to a new string directly, it finds the object from the pool, if already existing in the pool, and returns that object reference for the new variable. However this does not happen if the new operator is used. In that case it creates a new String anyway.

Since the == operator actually compares the reference of two objects, in the second case, they being the same (referring to the same object) it returns true. However in the first case they are different object's references (underlying objects are different). Hence it returns false.

In the third case, the equals method actually compares the content of the String objects rather than the reference. Hence even though they are different objects, their contents being same, it returns true.

Q31. Provided str is a string variable, what is the difference between the following -

(a) "JOHN".equals(str)

(b) str.equals("JOHN")

Which one is preferrable?

A. (a) is preferrable as it will not throw NullPointerException. The literal "JOHN" is not null. Hence calling *equals* on that string does not throw the exception. However at the point of calling, if str holds no value (if it is null), then calling equals on that will result in NullPointerException. In this sense (a) is safer.

Q32. What does intern method of String class do?

A. String class maintains a pool of String objects. String being immutable, this helps reduce the memory footprint by avoiding creation of duplicate String objects of same value unnecessarily. When intern method is invoked on a string (e.g. str.intern()), equals() method is internally invoked to see if the string (string object with the same value) already exists in the pool.

If it does, the existing string is returned. Otherwise the string object (str) is added to the pool and a reference to this object is returned.

Q33. Is String thread safe?

A. Yes. Every immutable object in Java is thread safe. String being immutable, is thread safe.

Q34. If String is immutable, how would you go about concatenating to a String multiple times ?

A. A very simple answer to the question would be – to use StringBuffer or StringBuilder class, and to use the append function (available in either class) in order to concatenate strings.

However if the result of the concatenation is a literal, that is fully known at compile time, JVM will optimise it to create a single String object. Hence it may be better to use plane concatenation (that would possibly be simpler from code readability point of view).

Q35. What is the difference between StringBuffer and StringBuilder?

A. This is also possibly a favourite question with many interviewers. String being immutable, involved and especially repetitive String concatenations may be helped by using objects of either of the classes StringBuffer or StringBuilder. However StringBuilder is not thread safe (Stringbuffer is). For this reason, if thread safety is not specifically required, it is better to use StringBuilder instead of StringBuffer for reduced performance overhead.

String functions

A few questions about string functions.

Q36. What will the following result in ?

```
//------------------------
public class Test {

        public static void main(String[] args) {
                String str = "superman";
                System.out.println(str.substring(1,5));
        }
}
//------------------------
        given alternatives
        (a) does not compile
        (b) prints
        super
        (c) prints
        uper
        (d) prints
        uperm
```

For people who do not use these kind of String operations regularly, (or are not in touch with those particular methods), confusions may arise from quite a few angles here.

(1) Whether the first position in the string (first character) is indicated by 0 or 1?

(2) Whether the second argument indicates end index or length of the substring

(3) Whether both the start index and end index (if the second argument is end index) is inclusive or exclusive (i.e. whether end index 5 means, up to 5th position, or up to and including 5th position)

(4) And perhaps whether the function is substring or subString (with a capital S as the 4th character).

The response to these points are important (especially for the last two points), as they have general bearing on a lot of string functions. So once you know them, you may make good guess at similar questions involving other functions.

Let me respond in reverse. (4) as far as function names are concerned, almost all such functions with complete words have usual java convention (i.e. initCaps for words in the middle). However substring as I know is the only exception (which has all smallcase). [Incidentally 'concat' is a function with all small case letters (but it does not have complete words)]

In contrast to substring, both 'toString' and 'subSequence' maintains the general convention.

(3) In such functions in general, start index is inclusive and end index is exclusive. This can greatly help finding the result of more complex string manipulations involving multiple functions.

(2) In such functions in general, index and length are not mixed. So if the first one is index, the second one is also index.

And (1)the first position is indicated by 0. So substring(0,5) will not throw an error but include the first character in the result. Note that by the same logic, index 5 indicates 6th character. So end index 5 (end index is exclusive) means up to but not including 6th character.

In this case the correct choice is (c)

Q37. Write a program to convert the String "manbittenbyspider" to a string "Spiderman"
using String functions (and without directly assigning either the whole string or character by character?

A. this can be done in several ways. A couple of solutions are given below. Please note that, this kind of questions require recalling into memory, some string functions - including their name and what all arguments they take.

For these kind of impromptu conversion requirements, it may be advisable to familiarise yourself with a few functions and the arguments they take. The functions I would suggest is - replace, replaceAll, split, concat and substring(two variations).

Solution 1.
```
//-------------------------
public class Test {
        public static void main(String[] args) {
                String str = "manbittenbyspider";
                String rslt =
str.substring(11).concat(str.substring(0,3)).replace('s','S');
                System.out.println(rslt);
        }
}
//-------------------------
```

Solution 2.
```
//-------------------------
public class Test {
        public static void main(String[] args) {
                String str = "manbittenbyspider";
                String[] strArr = str.split("bittenby");
                String rslt =
strArr[1].concat(strArr[0]).replace('s','S');
                System.out.println(rslt);
        }
}
```

//-------------------------

Sometimes a question may come to figure out the result of a series of operations. For instance -

Q38. What is the outcome in the following case?

//-------------------------

```java
public class Test {
        public static void main(String[] args) {
                String str = "King and countery";
                String rslt =
                                str.replaceAll(" ", "")
                                .substring(4,15)
                                .replaceFirst("a","e")
                                .split("[xyz]")[0];
                System.out.println(rslt);
        }
}
```

//-------------------------

        alternatives
        (a) does not compile
        (b) runs and prints
        encounter
        (c) runs and prints
        endcounter
        (d) runs and prints
        endcountery

        The correct answer is choice (c). Note that split in this form takes a regular expression as an argument.

The following question may seriously question the general notion that there is no such question as a stupid question. But this too may have a purpose.

Q39. What is the outcome in the following case?

```
//-------------------------
public class Test {
        public static void main(String[] args) {
                String str = "King";
                System.out.println(str.reverse(3,1));

        }
}
//-------------------------
        alternatives
        (a) does not compile
        (b) runs and prints
        gni
        (c) runs and prints
        gniK
        (d) runs and prints
        nik
```

The correct answer is choice (a). There is no reverse function (as yet) in String class. However, for someone not very familiar with the kind of functions String class have, it may be tempting to think that such a function may exist (wouldn't it be nice!). On top of that when there are arguments to the function and three of the answers are pointing to different combination of characters, the focus may easily shift to a mathematical attempt to figure out which combination should be correct, if there were such a function.

The real test here is, of course, how familiar one is with

different String functions available.

Q40. What is the outcome of the following code ?
```
//-------------------------
public class Test {
        public static void main(String[] args) {
                String str = "abc";
                System.out.println(str.substring(0,0).isEmpty());
        }
}
//-------------------------
```
alternatives

(a) does not compile

(b) throws NullPointerException

(c) runs and prints
true

(d) runs and prints
false

This is a bit of a twister. Although start Index is inclusive and end Index is exclusive in general, when both indexes are same, the exclusivity takes over, i.e. the length of the returned sub-string becomes zero.

Hence the above code will print true. Correct choice is (c).

A little bit of formatting may also come handy. For instance,

Q41. suppose a double variable named pi has a value 3.1415926. Write a piece of code to print the value up to two decimal places.

A.
```
//-------------------------
```

```
public class Test {
        public static void main(String[] args) {
                double pi = 3.1415926;
                System.out.println(String.format("%.2f", pi));
        }
}
//-------------------------
```

Contract for key objects

Q42. If someone defines a class, to be used for the key of a HashMap, what are the method/methods that he would usually override?

　　　alternatives

　　　(a) hashCode and equals

　　　(b) equals

　　　(c) finalize

　　　(d) toString

　　　Correct choice here is (a). As per the contract for hashCode and equals, when one is overridden, the other should also be overridden to define a custom key object.

　　　This question may come in many flavours such as -

A developer has overridden two methods of Object class in order to define a class for key objects. One of them is equals, what is the other method?

Q43. Of the following two classes, Ky is designed to be the key for a HashMap used in the Test class.

```
//----------------------------------
```

```java
public class Ky {
    private String str;
    public Ky(String str) {
        this.str = str;
    }
    public String getStr() {
        return str;
    }
    public void setStr(String str) {
        this.str = str;
    }

    public int hashCode() {
        return str.hashCode();
    }

    public boolean equals(Ky ky) {
        return this.equals(ky);
    }
}

public class Test {
    public static void main(String[] args) {
        Map<Ky, String> myMap = new HashMap<Ky, String>();

        Ky k1 = new Ky("abc");
```

```
Ky k2 = new Ky("def");
Ky k3 = new Ky("ghi");
Ky k4 = new Ky("abc");

myMap.put(k1,"1");
myMap.put(k2,"2");
myMap.put(k3,"3");
myMap.put(k4,"4");
System.out.println("size : " + myMap.size());
  }
}
//----------------------------------
```

What will happen if Test class is attempted to run ?

alternatives

(a) results in compilation error

(b) runs and prints

size : 3

(c) runs and prints

size : 4

(d) results in runtime error

The correct choice is (c) here.

That is because the override of equals method, which happens on the equals method of the Object class takes a parameter of type Object.

i.e. public boolean equals(Object arg1)

In our case the equals method takes parameter of type Ky, which makes the method signature different. So it is not the same method any more (and hence overriding does not occur). While comparing keys, k1 and k4 are treated as different objects and both gets places in the map. Hence the size turns out to be 4.

Q44. What would happen, if in the above code, the methods hasCode and equals are annotated with @Override?

   alternatives

   (a) results in compilation error

   (b) runs and prints

   size : 3

   (c) runs and prints

   size : 4

   (d) results in runtime error

In this case (especially if equals method has the annotation), the code will not compile correctly. That is because the compiler becomes aware that this is supposed to be a overridden method from a superclass (in this case Object). However the method signature in this class, does not match the method signature of the superclass. Hence it will result in compilation error. The correct choice is (c).

Q45. What if @Override annotation was added to the two methods, and the signature of equals was changed to accept a parameter of type Object. i.e. that part of the code was changed to -

   @Override

   public int hashCode() {

```
    return str.hashCode();
}


@Override
public boolean equals(Object ky) {
    return this.equals(ky);
}
```

alternatives

(a) results in compilation error

(b) runs and prints

size : 3

(c) runs and prints

size : 4

(d) results in runtime error

It results in runtime error, specifically StackOverflowError. That is because equals function now ends up being a recursive function with no proper terminating condition.

Q46. What if that portion of the code were to change to -

```
public int hashCode() {
    return str.hashCode();
}


public boolean equals(Object ky) {
    return this.str.equals(((Ky)ky).getStr());
```

}

alternatives

(a) results in compilation error

(b) runs and prints

size : 3

(c) runs and prints

size : 4

(d) results in runtime error

The correct choice in this case is (b). This, in some sense is the desired form of code (although the equals function is incomplete in some sense), if Ky is to be used as a class for HashMap keys where comparison of value in the String member determines whether it is the same key or not. Note that the same functionality could be achieved in this case, by using String as the key type rather than Ky.

Q47. For overridden equals method, in order to check whether the passed argument is an object of same type (as the current object), which one is better - instanceof or getClass ?

A. getClass. That is because instanceof check will not correctly identify a class in case of class hierarchies. For instance if Truck is a subclass of Car, then an instance of Truck is also an instance of Car. Hence, for a stricter check getClass is better.

The following code -

//----------------------------------

```
public class Test {
    public static void main(String[] args) {
```

```java
        Car car = new Car();
        Truck truck = new Truck();
        if (truck instanceof Car)
            System.out.println("truck is a Car");
        else
            System.out.println("truck is not a Car");


        System.out.println("className : " +
truck.getClass().getName());


    }
}
//----------------------------------
        runs and prints -
        truck is a Car
        className : Truck
```

However so long as such explicit hierarchies do not exist (or does not matter for comparison, even if it does exist), instanceof can be used in equals.

Q48. What will happen if the Test class is attempted to run given the following code

```java
//----------------------------------
public class Ky {
    private String str;
    private static int count = 0;
```

```java
    public Ky(String str) {
        this.str = str;
    }
    public String getStr() {
        return str;
    }

    public int hashCode() {
        count++;
        return count % 4 ;
    }

    public boolean equals(Object ky) {
        return this.str.equals(((Ky)ky).getStr());
    }
}

public class Test {
    public static void main(String[] args) {
        Map<Ky, String> myMap = new HashMap<Ky, String>();

        Ky k1 = new Ky("abc");
        Ky k2 = new Ky("def");
        Ky k3 = new Ky("ghi");
        Ky k4 = new Ky("abc");
```

```java
        myMap.put(k1,"1");
        myMap.put(k2,"2");
        myMap.put(k4,"4");

        System.out.println("size : " + myMap.size());
        System.out.println("hashCode : " + k4.hashCode());
        System.out.println("value : " + myMap.get(k4));


    }
}
//--------------------------------
        alternatives
        (a) results in compilation error
        (b) runs and prints
        size : 2
        hashCode : 1
        value : null
        (c) runs and prints
        size : 3
        hashCode : 0
        value : 1
        (d) runs and prints
        size : 2
        hashCode : 0
        value : null
```

The correct choice here is (c).

In a HashMap hashcode is used to determine the bucket and equals is used to make a more precise judgement of element within a bucket.

Everytime *put* is called, determination is required as to which bucket it will go into, and hence, hashCode function will be called. If the bucket is empty however, there is no need to call *equals*, as there will be no conflict for place. [A Map keeps only one copy of an object (uniqueness being judged by key)].

While *get* is called however, it has to first narrow down the search by determining the bucket in which the object exists (if at all). Hence a call to hashCode function is made. However, even as the bucket is found, the exact object (as judged by key) still needs to be identified. As the bucket may have more than one object, equals function is needed to identify the exact one.

On top of that, the hashCode function has been called explicitly on the k4 object in the code. So by the time the get function internally calls hashCode function it will be the fifth call to that function.

For the initial *put* k1 has the hashCode 1. On the 5th call, k4 will return the same hashcode. Upon that, when equals function is called, k1, and k4 both have the same value for the String member, making them same object from equals function's point of view. So k4 will be deemed the same object as k1 at this point, and the HashMap will come up with the value correspoding to String "1".

For a demonstartion, if you change the two functions to print messages (as shown below) -

```
public int hashCode() {
  System.out.println("hashCode called");

  count++;

  return count % 4 ;

}
```

```
public boolean equals(Object ky) {
    System.out.println("equals called");
    return this.str.equals(((Ky)ky).getStr());
}
```

and run the code, the output should reflect the calls to those functions (implicit or explicit) and it will be -

hashCode called

hashCode called

hashCode called

size : 3

hashCode called

hashCode : 0

hashCode called

equals called

value : 1

Try putting one more object in the first bucket, and try to see what happens on call to hashCode and equals functions for the *put* of that object.

Mixed topic 1

A job interview is different from a boxing match, (although sometimes it may feel that way to some interviewees), in many ways. One of them being that, the interviewer is not bound by the same set of rules as may be applied (rather implicitly) or assumed for the interviewee. One possible outcome of that is, a question need not be bound to a single topic. Mix and match of very wild variety may occur. One example of that mix and match is the following question.

Q49. What is the difference between final, finally and finalize ?

By my own experience and studies, it seems to be a favourite question with many interviewers. However, even though the question is of a mix and match variety, this is a good question as far as interview questions go, as a basic filtering between people who know their trade (of Java programming) and people who don't (people who are plane lucky etc. are excluded from this context).

A. It draws on three different aspects of Java programming. The keyword *final is a modifier (of a variable, a method, or a class)*. The keyword *finally is a block identifier in exception handling construct (more precisely try-catch-finally construct)*, and *finalize is a method of object class, which may be overridden (usually to release or terminate resources)*.

It is possible that a follow up question may follow the trail of one of these three keywords. For instance -

Q50. What is the use of final keyword in context of methods, classes and variables?

A. A final class can not be extended or subclassed. A final method can not be overridden in a subclass when the corresponding class is extended, and a final variable can not be reassigned after it's initial assignment.

Q51. What will the following code result in ?
//----------------------------------

```
public class Test {
    public static void main(String[] args) {
        Object obj1 = String.class;
        System.out.println("Object 1 : " + obj1);
    }
}
//----------------------------------
```

The set of alternatives

(a) Does not compile successfully

(b) runs and prints -

Object 1 : class java.lang.String

(c) runs and prints -

Object 1 : String@9375

This may seem baffling at first. And if such a question is asked towards the beginning of an interview, and the answer is not known, it may ruin the whole interview.

Constructs such as String.class denotes a *Class* type object (and is therefore an object). Think of a pottery mould, in which you can put clay and get a 3d object made of clay, such as a flower vase. The vases are objects. However the mould itself is also a physical object, of a different kind.

Therefore it is perfectly legal to assign a Class type object to a variable of type Object. As for the print, that too is legal, and (b) is the correct choice in this case.

Orientation to objects

Java being an object oriented programming language (whatever that means), an interview for a Java Developer position is quite likely to involve questions on object orientation. Some of the questions may be more generic, on the basic concepts of object orientation, and some other may involve object orientation as applied to Java in particular. Some questions may be mixed and some may go in a roundabout way.

It is perhaps relevant to understand some basics such as -

Q52. What are the main features that make a language object oriented?

A. Remember the word PIE. Polymorphism, Inheritance and Encapsulation.

Objects use Encapsulation (of data and operations), one Class (usually) can be inherited by ity's subclasses (which extends it), which therefore can extend it's behaviour (among other things). And Polymorphism provides a way to modify a known behaviour in a subclass (or any class below in the hierarchy of extension – so long as the method has not been declared *final*, before that).

One popular question in this category is -
Q53. What is the difference between overloading and overriding ?

A. This is again a mix and match question, but a good one.

Overriding is the mechanism by which polymorphism in Java takes place. It is redefining the same function in the subclasses (or child classes) to have different behaviour (different code body). For instance a class *Shape* may have a *draw* function, which may be empty. Whereas, two of it's child classes, *Square* and *Circle*, may override the *draw* function, to draw corresponding shapes.

Overloading on the other hand is, using the same function name, but different set of parameters, two create multiple functions of same name, which in Java way are actually different functions. So a draw function which takes no argument is different from a draw function in the same class which takes for instance an *int* as an argument. In this case the draw function is overloaded. [It is possible that it is due to a lack of imagination on the part of designer or developer, that for different kinds of behaviour, different names could not be found. However it is also possible that there was a good case for actually defining two functions with same name but different parameters].

Incidentally, in Java the return type is not considered part of the function signature, while judging uniqueness of functions. Hence two functions having same name, and same set of arguments will clash even if their return type is different.

Q54. What is the difference between interfaces and abstract classes ?

Apparently this too is a popular one among Java interviewers. This also reflects some basic understanding, or the lack of it, in basic object oriented concepts.

There may be many points that can be stated as differentiating interfaces and abstract classes, but the answer, even in brief should include something that shows that the candidate understands what they are. Also, this question, at least some of the time, may come with the expectation that the similarities of the two are also discussed.

A. [Note interfaces have changed in Java 8. But this answer is relevant before that. The main change in Java 8 being, it allows static and default methods (with method body) in interfaces].

An interface structurally is a reference type (like class), and functionally a class template or desired class specification, which can only contain constants, method signatures and nested types. Whereas an abstract class is a class with at least one abstract method.

One of the similarities being neither an interface nor an abstract class can be instantiated.

An abstract class, being a class, is extended (with the extends keyword) whereas an interface is implemented (with the implements keyword).

(a similarity) Any concrete (non-abstract) class that extends the abstract class, has to implement the abstract method(s). And any concrete class that implements an interface also has to implement the methods whose signature is specified in the interface.

A class can only extend from one abstract class, but can implement multiple inheritances.

(Going further into the nitty gritty), you can have private members in an abstract class but you can not have private variables in interfaces. Also all interface variables are static and final by default.

(one important point about the usage) An abstract class is generally chosen where a lot of the behaviour of the classes that would extend it, is already known/fixed. So only the part that differs from class to class can be kept abstract and later implemented in the concrete classes. In this sense an abstract class is more like a partially built machine. Whereas an interface is more like a specification without implementation, (like an electrical plug point specification, where any appliance with conforming plug can be used). In this sense it is more like a behavioural blueprint of the machine to be built (without almost any part having actually been in place).

Exception handling

Q55. Can a try block exist without a corresponding catch block.

A. This is a tricky question and the answer is yes. The condition is, a try block must have at least a corresponding *catch or finally* block. Hence a try with a corresponding finally block (without a catch block) is perfectly legal. Although, if not known or thought through before, this question may cause confusion.

Q56a. With respect to the following code (two classes), what happens if one tries to run the Test class ?

```
//---------------------------------
public class Car {
  public static int count() {
    try {
      System.out.println("A");
      System.exit(0);
      return 1;
    } finally {
      System.out.println("B");
      return 2;
    }
  }
}

public class Test {
    public static void main(String[] args) {
      System.out.println("Count : " + Car.count());
    }
}
//-------------------------------
```

alternatives

(a) does not compile

(b) runs and prints

A

Count : 0

(c) runs and prints

A

B

Count : 2

(c) runs and prints

A

Count : 1

       There is no statement which may lead to compilation error. Also the argument to exit is for the outer shell, not for the Java class with the main function. Hence the o (zero) of the exit will not feature in the output here. It will exit from the try block at the exit call. The correct choice is (b).

Q56b. What happens when the following is attempted to run ?

```
//----------------------------------
public class Car {
  public static int count() {
     try {
        System.out.println("A");
        return 1;
     } finally {
        System.out.println("B");
        return 2;
     }
  }
}


public class Test {
    public static void main(String[] args) {
      System.out.println("Count : " + Car.count());
    }
}
//----------------------------------
        alternatives
```

(a) does not compile

(b) runs and prints

A

Count : 1

(c) runs and prints

A

B

Count : 2

Short of exit or such like, finally block always executes after try. In this case also, finally will execute and the function count will return 2. The correct choice is (c).

Q57. Can you declare a function as throwing a RuntimeException?

A. Yes. Although not usually done, it is perfectly legal to have a function declare to be throwing a runtime exception e.g.

```
//-----------------------
public static int count() throws NullPointerException {
        return 1;
}
//-----------------------
```

Q58. What happens if a function declares throwing a runtime exception and the calling function does not catch it. e.g.

```
//-----------------------
public class Car {
  public static int count() throws NullPointerException {
    return 1;
  }
}
```

```java
public class Test {
   public static void main(String[] args) {
     System.out.println("Count : " + Car.count());
   }
}
}
//-----------------------
```

        alternatives

        (a) does not compile

        (b) Works as usual

        A runtime exception is not mandatory to catch. Hence it will work as usual (unless of course there is error). Correct choice is (b).

Q59. What is the Exception hierarchy in Java ?

        A. at the root of the hierarchy is Throwable (class) which has Error and Exception as it's subclasses. Exception further subclasses into other (checked) exceptions and RuntimeException class. RuntimeException is the root class of all runtime (unchecked exceptions).

```
Throwable ->
        Error ->
        Exception ->
                IOException
                ...
                RuntimeException ->
                        NullPointerException
                        ...
```

Q60. What are the different types of Exceptions?

A. Although the question could have been specified better, some interviewer may ask the question exactly that way, and the usual expectation is, you talk about checked and unchecked exceptions. And when you do, add a sentence or two about what they are.

Exceptions are of two types, checked exceptions and unchecked exceptions. Checked exceptions are checked at compile time, and unchecked exceptions are not. They occur at runtime.

Q61. Name two checked exceptions other than IOException or Exception, and two unchecked Exceptions other than RuntimeException or NullPointerException ?

A. Even for an experienced Java programmer, recalling a few exception names quickly from memory may not be easy. So it is a good idea, to keep a few handy, for quick recall.

checked : SQLException, JAXBException

unchecked : NumberFormatException, ArrayIndexOutOfBoundsException

Note : when someone mentions these or any other exceptions, as an answer to this question, it may invoke further questions on one of those exceptions - in terms of - in what scenario such exceptions occur ?

Q62. What are the differences between checked and unchecked exceptions?

A. I would guess this too is somewhat of a favourite with many interviewers.

(a) Checked exceptions are checked at compile time and unchecked exceptions are not.

(b) Throwing a checked exception usually indicates that the caller can recover from it. Unchecked exceptions on the other hand comes with the expectation that the caller will not be able to recover from it.

(c) All checked exceptions are derived from Exception or it's subclasses (except RuntimeException). All unchecked exceptions are derived one way or another from RuntimeException.

Miscellaneous

Q63. What does transient modifier do ?

A. It indicates that the variable (which is marked transient) need not be serialized when an object of the class is serialized. For those variables state is not deemed important (important enough for it to be serialized). It could, for instance, be an intermediate value in a process of calculations, which has importance only during the calculation process.

Q64. What is marker interface ? Provide an example of implementation in Java ?

A. A marker interface follows marker interface design pattern, which (usually) provides a means to associate meta-data information with a class, where the language does not have such mechanism.

Such interfaces usually does not have any methods. The very presence of such an interface indicates that the class implementing it should conform to certain specific behaviour.

Serializable interface in Java is an example of marker interface implementation. When a class implements Serializable, it declares (or that is the expectation), that it is safe to serialize the class. The writeObject() method of the ObjectOutputStream class, checks among other things, whether the class (which is supposed to be serialized) implements the Serializable interface. If not, it raises NotSerializableException.

Collection classes

Q65. What happens if you try to remove an element from a list, that you are traversing through with an iterator ?

A. ConcurrentModificationException will result.

Q66. Suppose you have a list of Strings, from which you want to remove any element which holds the string "Not Required". Write a piece of code to demonstrate how you would do it. (Suppose the list is named strLst and is already populated).

A.

```
Iterator<String> it = strLst.iterator();
while(it.hasNext()) {
        String str = it.next();
        if("Not Required".equals(str))
                it.remove();
}
```

Note that this is a solution for a single-threaded program. However if the question does not mention multi-threaded environment, assume single threaded.

In case of multi-threaded code, CopyOnWriteArrayList (concurrent collection class) may be used.

Multi-threading

Q67. What is the difference between a process and a thread ?

A. The main difference between a process and a thread is that a process has it's own execution environment including memory space of it's own, whereas threads share a common memory space.

Thus a thread may be less expensive in terms of resources.

A process may contain multiple threads.

Q68. How do you make sure that a piece of code that is supposed to be run for one thread at a time (as an unit), runs in that manner in a multi-threaded program.

A. The code may be put in a method or a block, which may be synchronized using the *synchronized* keyword. e.g

public synchronized int nextval() {

return count++;

}

Q69. Can a class be synchronized?

A. No. Only a method or a block can be synchronized.

Q70. An Int variable count, needs to be incremented in a synchronized block so that only one object at a time can increment it. How should the block code look like.

A. [This question may be asked to get a demonstration from the candidate that he knows the syntax for the synchronized block.]

synchronized (this) {

count++;

}

Synchronizing on *this* will ensure that the piece of code is executed by one object at a time (when the class runs as threads).

Q71. If a block is synchronized on the class e.g.

synchronized (Car.class) {

...

}

what does that imply?

A. It implies that the lock is held on the class object. Stating in another way – the object of monitor for the synchronization in this case is the Class object for the class.

In effect it is somewhat like synchronizing a static method.

Q72. Suppose in a class there are two non static synchronized methods a and b. When a thread is executing the method a, can another thread execute the method b?

A. No. For a non static synchronized method, the object of monitor is *this* (the object on which the method was invoked). And the object of monitor is the same (instance) for both the methods. Hence when one method is invoked, the monitor for that instance is already acquired by that thread, and other threads can not get hold of the same instance monitor, unless this thread releases the lock.

Q73. How can you create an instance of a Thread ?

A. There are two ways in which a class can be directly made multi-threaded (create an instance of a Thread). By extending the Thread class and by implementing the Runnable interface. Of which the second approach is more generic (normally), as it allows the class to subclass a class other than the Thread class.

Q74. In a multi-threaded context, what will happen if the run method is called directly on the Thread object, instead of the start method ?

A. That will cause the code specified in the run method, to execute in the current thread, without creating a new thread.

Q75. Why are *wait* and *notify*, methods of the Object class (instead of Thread class)?

A. In a multi-threaded environment, wait happens on a particular monitor, assigned to an object. If you want to send a notification to a single thread that is waiting on that particular object instance, then you call notify on that object. If all threads, that are waiting on that particular object instance are to be notified, notifyAll method on that object should be called.

an Object thus (more precisely the monitor assigned to the object), is treated as a means of communication among threads, for coordination of activities. A thread, being a lightweight mechanism for parallelism, need not have specific knowledge of other threads that it has to wait on (if it had to then all threads would require being registered, and you would need to call thread1.wait() or thread5.notify() as the case may be. That would make threads expensive to maintain, and creation of new threads cumbersome), it just needs to keep track of the monitor for coordination.

Hence those methods are better off in Object class than in Thread class.

Q76. What is a volatile variable ?

A. A volatile variable is a variable which has only one copy across all the threads of the same class.

i.e. suppose a class has a private String member str1, and a volatile boolean variable vbool. If five objects of the class are created and running as different threads, there will be five str1 variables (one per object) but only one vbool (used across all five threads).

These variables can be used effectively, under some circumstances, to communicate status etc, across multiple threads.

Q77. How can you create daemon threads ?

A. A deamon thread can be created from a program by calling the setDaemon function passing true as argument, prior to calling start method on the thread.

t.setDaemon(true);

t.start();

Q78a. Is it possible that main function has exited, while threads created by the program is still running ?

A. Yes

Q78b. What function can you use to make sure that it does not happen ? (I.e. main thread is finished only after all non-daemon thread from the program has completed).

A. This can be done using the join function.

The method *join*, in it's plain form (without any argument) wait for the thread (on which the join method has been called) to die before the current thread resumes. If join on other threads are called from main thread (main function runs in main thread), then main thread has to wait for them to die/finish prior to it's own completion (unless of course program crashes etc.).

As an example, When you run the Test class as defined below [the code consists of two classes] -

```java
//---------------------------
public class Test {

    public static void main(String[] args) {
        MyThread mt1 = new MyThread(1);
        MyThread mt2 = new MyThread(2);

        System.out.println("From main thread : one");
        mt1.start();
        mt2.start();

        try {
            mt1.join();
            mt2.join();
        } catch (InterruptedException e) {
            e.printStackTrace();
        }

        System.out.println("From main thread : two");
    }
}

public class MyThread extends Thread {
```

```
        private int myId = 0;

        MyThread(int id) {
                myId = id;
        }

        @Override
        public void run() {
                System.out.println("From child thread : " +
myId);
        }

}
//- - - - - - - - - - - - - - - - - - - - - - - - -
```
        It should produce something like -
From main thread : one
From child thread : 1
From child thread : 2
From main thread : two

        Note that the ordering of 1 and 2 is not guaranteed.

Memory

Q79. Name two common types of OutOfMemoryError in Java.

        A. *java.lang.OutOfMemoryError: Java heap space* and
java.lang.OutOfMemoryError: PermGen space

        Note there are other types of OutOfMemoryError also.
However it would be good to mention these two.

Q80. Why does OutOfMemoryError: Java heap space happen ?
And what can you do to prevent it in your application ?

        A. As the application runs and different objects are
created, it takes up memory.

        Overall memory allocated to JVM has an upper bound
(could be parametrized or platform default), and so has *Java
heap space*, which is a part of the memory that keeps (roughly
speaking) objects and object data as opposed to class

definition/metadata, Java primitives, String pool etc. which are kept in PermGen space (which is another part of the memory and also has an upper bound).

Garbage Collection process in Java, reclaims the memory from objects that are no longer in use or referenced. However for some reason, if in spite of the garbage collection, there is not enough space available in the heap space part of the memory, to continue the operation of JVM, then this error will be thrown.

The underlying cause may be many. For instance the memory requirement of the application itself may not have been met. (i.e. the normal working of the application requires more memory than is allocated). Quite often however it may happen due to objects reference being kept alive unduly (when, for instance, the objects have served their purpose, and no longer required). It can also happen when many more users are using the application at once, than was originally anticipated (and designed for).

One way to stop this from happening is to increase the heap space allocation with the -Xmx option. However in case of underlying problem in code, such as too many undue references, this may be attacking the symptom rather than the core of the problem, and the problem may recur. So proper review and monitoring may be necessary to find the underlying cause. It is also possible that design review may be needed, for proper allocation of resources for peak usage of the application.

Q81. Why does OutOfMemoryError: PermGen space happen? And what can you do to prevent it in your application?

A. JVM uses *PermGen space* part of the memory for class meta-data, Java primitives, String pool etc. (Certain things that are more permanent, or definition related as opposed to object instances and running data). *Note Classses themselves are objects but they are for PermGen space.*

There is an upper bound to this space (which may be configured, or taken as platform default), and when the limit is exceeded the error is thrown.

Since the cause is, (roughly speaking), meta-data overflow - this can be caused by several underlying issues, such as too many classes being loaded, or too big classes being loaded, or String pool becoming too big due to a lot of big String literals, or the old classloader not being unloaded during redeployment of an application and so on – which causes the PermGen space to clog.

One solution could be to increase the upper bound of PermGen space using the -XX:MaxPermSize option (JVM option). However, under certain circumstances, that may mean treating the symptom rather than the real problem. The application may be monitored to see if old classloaders are being held unduly, during application redeployment, and appropriate measures taken to mitigate that (including code to deregister classes when the application context is destroyed).

Design Patterns

Q82. What is a design pattern (as applicable to software development) ?

A. Many problems in software development, within a given context, tend to follow certain pattern (For instance, only one instance of an object is necessary for an application, and the object is heavy, so unnecessary instantiation of multiple objects will be taxing on the resources). *A design pattern is a reusable generic solution template (or solution pattern) which addresses the solution to the problem pattern elegantly, (usually) following formalized best practices.* They are usually templates to show, what process and artefacts the solution should have, and their interrelationship, in order to tackle the problem, without the finished code. They focus specifically on that particular problem space, leaving out detail of any other functionality of the application, that is irrelevant to this particular problem space.

Q83. Name any three prominent design patterns. (It may also be asked as name three design patterns that you have used in course of software development).

A. [It is very likely that, whatever patterns you name, the interviewer is likely to question further on at least one of them. What they are and where they are used.

Also in case you have not used (at least consciously) enough design patterns yourself, I suggest you reply mentioning that you have not used but you are aware of many design patterns such as ...]

Singleton pattern, Abstract factory pattern, Adapter pattern.

Q84. What is Singleton design pattern ?

A. It is a design pattern where only one instance of the class is allowed in the whole context. *Please note that Singleton is Singleton in context of the classloader.*

Q85. What are the things you would follow to make a class Singleton ?

A. The constructor should be private and there should be a public method which will return an instance (or a reference thereof) of the class to clients (calling classes). This method should check whether an instance of the class already exists. If it does, it would return a reference to that instance. If it does not, it should first create an instance and then return a reference to the created instance.

Q86. What are the usual types of design patterns ?

A. Creational, Structural and Behavioural patterns.

Q 87. What is a Front Controller pattern ? Where is it used ?

A. Front Controller pattern deals with providing a centralized entry point for the requests. It's common use is in web applications.

Many web frameworks (such as Spring MVC) uses this pattern to route requests. In a Spring MVC application for instance, a DispatcherServlet first receives the request and routes it to appropriate resources for handling. It also routes the final response to the client.

Q88. What is Flyweight pattern ? What is it's usage?

A. A *Flyweight* is an object that shares data with similar objects in order to reduce memory footprint. Quite often a large number of objects can share states, and simple instantiation of the objects will create replicated states, which may demand unacceptable amount of memory. In such cases, the shareable states can be held in external data structures and passed to the flyweight objects temporarily as required.

String interning in Java, is a good example of the implementation of that pattern.

Q89. What is dependency Injection ?

A. Dependency injection is a design pattern, that embodies Inversion of Control principle, in order to decouple dependencies between components. It involves injecting (passing by reference) of dependencies (services) into a dependent object (client), which (the reference to the service) then are made part of the client's state. Thus development of functionality of the service, is decoupled from development of other parts of clients own behaviour.

For instance, reference to a DAO object (specialized for data access) may be injected in a client, which may drain some data by calling methods on the reference, do it's own calculation, and call another method on the reference, to persist the result of the calculation. The developer of the client class need not bother with the internals of the persistence mechanism. He needs to focus mainly on the correctness of the calculation, and calling the data access and persistence methods in appropriate order.

Q90. What are the different types of dependency injection ?

A. Three types of dependency injections are in common use. Setter injection, constructor injection and interface injection.

Setter Injection works through injecting a dependency through the setter method of the client. Constructor injection works through passing the dependency as an argument to the constructor of the client. Whereas in interface injection, the client implements an interface, which has a setter method for injecting the dependency.

Data structures

Q91. What will the following code result in -

```
//-----------------------------------
public class Test {
    public static void main(String[] args) {
        int a[] = {};
        a[0] = 1;
        System.out.println("1st element : " + a[0]);
    }
}
//-----------------------------------
```

The set of alternatives

(a) Does not compile successfully

(b) results in exception at runtime

(c) runs and prints -

1st element : 1

A. The array has been initialized, but with an empty array (array of zero elements). The index for access won't be validated until runtime. But at run time it will throw ArrayIndexOutOfBoundsException. The correct answer is (b).

Note however that if you change the line of array declaration to

int a[];

then it won't compile, as array has not been initialized.

Q92. Suppose you have a requirement to store scientific names of different animals, so that given the usual name of the animal, such as horse, you can easily get the scientific name. What data structure would you use?

A. Map is the general data structure that should be used in this situation. More specifically Map<String, String> and the implementation HashMap may be used.

Q93. What is the difference between HashMap and TreeMap ?

A. A HashMap is a Hash based Map implementation (easy to remember) more specifically a HashMap in Java is a *Hash table implementation of the Map interface*. Whereas a TreeMap is a Tree based Map implementation. More specifically a TreeMap is a *Red-black tree implementation of the SortedMap interface*.

In TreeMap, keys can be sorted, and while iterating, traversal can happen in order of the keys. No such guarantee for HashMap. However HashMap is more efficient in general.

Also TreeMap works with Comparable objects, whereas

for HashMap (for custom key objects), equals and HashCode methods need to be overridden.

Q94. An Array of Strings contains duplicate elements as shown below.

String[] strArr = {"Car", "Truck", "Bike", "Car", "Vehicle"};

A programmer has written a class, with nested for loop, to eliminate the duplicates. What data structure can you use to make the duplicate ellimination more efficient?

A. Set.

Q95. How can you create or populate a List of Strings with elements from a set (of Strings) without using for loop ?

A. Suppose the name of the set is strSet. The following would do the job.

List<String> lstStr = new ArrayList<String>(strSet);

Q96. While checking whether there is any element in a list, a programmer is doing the following -

if (strLst.size() > 0) {

(where strLst is the name of the List), could you do better ?

A. Yes. The isEmpty() method should be called on the list instead of size(). This is because, the size function will traverse the whole list, while isEmpty will return much quicker (possibly returning upon checking the first element if there is any).

Note : depending on implementation of List, size could also be fast, but isEmpty should be more sensible choice still, because – (1) if you depend on size for this purpose, you tie the performance to implementation (2) isEmpty is a more explicit description of the objective in this case.

Q97. How can you sort a list without using for loop?

A. Collections.sort(strLst)

where strLst is the name of the list.

Q98. What is the difference between ArrayList and LinkedList ?

A. Usually the type of data structures that are easier to retrieve from, are the ones which are more expensive for insert operations (and possibly also for removal) and vice versa.

ArrayList is an array based (and hence position indexed) implementation of the List interface (more precisely *Resizable-array implementation of the List interface*). Wheras LinkedList is a *Doubly-linked list implementation of the List interface*.

Being what they are, ArrayLists are very efficient in index based search ($O(1)$) where as LinkedList may require cosiderable linear traversal ($O(n)$).

Insertion and deletion on the other hand are much faster with LinkedList. In LinkedList a deletion would involve unchaining and re-chaining two pointers (preceding and following neighbours of the deleted element). Whereas in ArrayList, based on where the element is being removed from, all susbequent elements may be required to be shifted in order to fill out the space created by the deleted element [worst case $O(n)$].

In terms of memory requirement, other than the element itself, an ArrayList has to maintain the index, and a LinkedList has to maintain two pointers (at least for the elements in the middle). Hence LinkedList is slightly heavier on that front.

Inner Classes

Q99. What in your view is closest to function pointers in Java ? And where are they commonly used ?

A. Anonymous inner classes.

They can be used in places where (usually) only a single instance of the object is required with a method overloaded. There use makes the coding quicker by not having to subclass the class for (usually) a single piece of functionality being overridden.

They are quite often used in ActionListeners in Swing.

Q100. Why are only final members of the outer class accessible to an anonymous inner class ?

A. Java does not have closures. The methods in an anonymous inner class don't really have access to the member variables of the outer class. Rather when an object of the inner class is instantiated, Java runtime makes a copy of the member variable (of the outer class), and the inner class instance accesses that copy. If the access were allowed to non final outer member variables, then changes to the member variable were possible in the outer class, independently of the value that was provided to the inner class instance, and that would create inconsistency. Hence ...

Q101. What is a member class ?

A. A member class is a named non-static inner class, that is defined within an outer class, at the member level, i.e. within the class but not within any method or block. e.g.

class MyOuter {

    class MyInner {

    }

}

Such a class can not be instantiated without instantiating the outer class.

```
finally {
        contact :
        samemalay@gmail.com
}
```

www.ingramcontent.com/pod-product-compliance
Lightning Source LLC
Chambersburg PA
CBHW061014050326
40689CB00012B/2636